To:

From:

For this child I prayed.

—1 Samuel 1:27 AMP

Forever My Little Boy

Forever My Little Boy
Loving Your Son for Now and for Always

KAREN KINGSBURY

Illustrated by Joanne Lew-Vriethoff

ZONDERVAN®

Dedicated to . . .
Donald, my Prince Charming,
Kelsey, my precious daughter,
Tyler, my beautiful song,
Sean, my wonder boy,
Josh, my tender tough guy,
EJ, my chosen one,
Austin, my miracle child,
and to God Almighty, the Author of life,
who has—for now—blessed me with these.

———

Mattiece, forever and ever.

—Joanne

One day a little boy was born into the world, and for a very small moment, his parents held him close.

But soon the doctor came for him, and right then his parents knew: life with that little boy would always mean letting him go.

I prayed for this child, and the Lord answered my prayer
and gave him to me. Now I give him back to the Lord. He
will belong to the Lord all his life.

—1 Samuel 1:27–28

Kind heavenly Father,

Thank You for this amazing gift—our baby boy.

You have entrusted him into our care.

Now help us to guide him.

Amen.

How quickly the baby boy became a one-year-old. He didn't want to be held anymore—he wanted to walk.

So Mom got the camera, Dad knelt down, and they held their breath. Then crookedly, very crookedly, their boy took his first steps.

From the place where she watched him, his mother hummed a quiet hum . . .

Forever, little boy,

Don't you fall, little boy.

Look how much you've grown.

Stay near, little boy, when you walk, little boy.

You're not yet on your own.

Dear God,

Bless our little boy with the gift of faith.

Lead him to walk with You in faith and

to trust Jesus as his Lord and Savior.

Amen.

I am guiding you in the way of wisdom,

and I am leading you on the right path.

Nothing will hold you back;

you will not be overwhelmed.

—Proverbs 4:11–12

Soon the boy was running everywhere, all the way through his preschool years. On his sixth birthday he got a shiny bike.

His father knew it was time to let go a little more. So he patted his son on his helmet, stood back, and slowly, very slowly, the boy climbed onto the seat.

From the place where he watched his son, the father whistled a quiet whistle . . .

Forever, little boy,
Do your best, little boy.
Look how much you've grown.
Be brave, little boy, while you try, little boy.
You're barely on your own.

Lord of all strength,

Please bless our little boy with perseverance.

Help him to always do his best,

and when he fails, enable him to try again.

Amen.

Train children to live the right way,

and when they are old, they will not stray from it.

—Proverbs 22:6

Years passed, and the boy became a fourth grader.

His mother knew it was time for him to walk to school by himself. So she kissed him good-bye, stood back, and watched as he quickly ran to meet his friends.

From the place where she watched him, his mother sang a quiet song . . .

Forever, little boy,

Be safe, little boy.

Look how much you've grown.

Be safe, little boy, wherever you go, little boy.

You'll soon be on your own.

Heavenly Father,
Wherever our boy goes, hold him close
and keep him forever in Your sight.
Protect our little boy when he is away from us,
and shelter him from harm.
Amen.

He has put his angels in charge of you

to watch over you wherever you go.

—Psalm 91:11

In middle school the boy became a football player.

Football was rough and tough and dangerous, but his father knew it was time to let him play. So he helped him with his shoulder pads, wished him good luck, and watched from the top of the bleachers. And wildly, very wildly, the boy tackled and ran.

From the place where his father watched him, he thought a quiet thought . . .

Forever, little boy,

Don't get hurt, little boy.

Look how much you've grown.

Play smart, little boy, when you play, little boy.

You're not quite on your own.

"Because he loves me," says the LORD, "I will rescue him;

I will protect him, for he acknowledges my name."

—Psalm 91:14 NIV

Dear God,

It is difficult to let go. Our boy is growing up.

When he plays, he plays hard, and he plays to win.

Lord, help him to play smart. Help him to play safe.

Amen.

When he became a teenager, he couldn't wait to learn to drive. Of course, his driving was scary for his parents.

Even so, they told him to be careful, watched from the top of the driveway, and carefully, very carefully, their boy backed the car down the hill and out of sight.

From the place where they watched him, his parents prayed a quiet prayer . . .

Forever, little boy,
Buckle up, little boy.
Look how much you've grown.
Take care, little boy, when you drive, little boy.
You're almost on your own.

Keep your eyes focused on what is right,

and look straight ahead to what is good.

—Proverbs 4:25

Lord of all,

Bless our son with the ability to make wise decisions,

and guard him from mindless distractions.

Lead him down right paths, now and forevermore.

Amen.

Now a young man, the boy fell in love.

His mother knew that she had to share her love for him with someone else. So she helped him order flowers, blew him a kiss as he drove off, and gladly, very gladly, he went to meet his girl.

From the place where she watched him go, his mother whispered a quiet whisper . . .

Forever, little boy,

Guard your heart, little boy.

Look how much you've grown.

Be with God, little boy, when you love, little boy,

Especially when on your own.

And the child grew and became strong; he was filled with wisdom, and the grace of God was on him.

—Luke 2:40 NIV

Great Provider,
We want our son to know love that is
true, right, and everlasting—
the kind of love that You have for him.
So, guide his heart. Lead him to the one
whom You've chosen for him.
Amen.

The boy made plans to marry and move away.

Marriage meant his parents might not see their boy much. But they knew their boy loved his girl, and it was time to plan a wedding. So they helped him find a fancy suit, and suddenly, very suddenly, their little boy was gone.

From the place where they watched him drive away from the church, his parents cried a heartfelt cry . . .

Forever, little boy,

Don't forget us, little boy,

As you head to your new home.

It's time, little boy, to let go, little boy.

You're fully on your own.

I trust God's love forever and ever.

—Psalm 52:8

God of all comfort,

We entrust our son to You today,

just as we have every day of his life.

Please bestow Your goodness upon him,

and fill his heart with Your love.

Amen.

A lifetime went by in the blink of an eye, and his parents grew old.

His mother had only a little while before God called her home to heaven. But she knew where she was going—and she told her boy so—when she called him to her side and said good-bye.

The boy leaned over and kissed her on the cheek, and barely, very barely, she squeezed his hand . . .

Forever, little boy,

Cling to God, little boy.

You'll never be alone.

In years to come, little boy, I'll be with you, little boy.

And one day we'll all be home.

The LORD bless you

and keep you;

the LORD make his face shine on you

and be gracious to you;

the LORD turn his face toward you

and give you peace.

—Numbers 6:24-26 NIV

Son, in our hearts you'll always be our little boy. At every age and every moment of life, know that you are cherished, prayed over, and oh so loved.

ALSO BY KAREN KINGSBURY

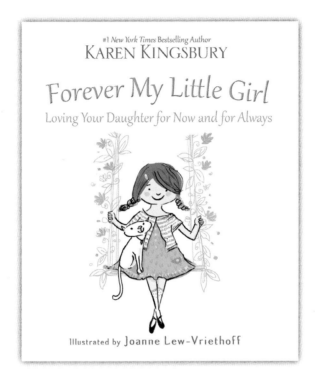

Even when our children grow up,
they always remain our little ones.

About #1 *New York Times* Bestselling Author

KAREN KINGSBURY

Karen Kingsbury, #1 *New York Times* bestselling novelist, is America's favorite inspirational storyteller, with more than 25 million copies of her award-winning books in print. Her last dozen titles have topped bestseller charts, and many of her novels are under development as major motion pictures with Hallmark. She lives in Tennessee with her husband, Don, and their five sons, three of whom are adopted from Haiti. Their actress daughter, Kelsey, lives nearby and is married to Christian recording artist Kyle Kupecky. The couple recently welcomed their first child, Hudson, making Karen and Don grandparents for the first time.